Love, Lust and Other Monsters
Inner Dialogue Series Book II

Purge, recycle, evolve and repeat...
Poems by Chara Ann Tappin-McCabe

All rights reserved. No part of this book may be reproduced or transmitted in any form or by any means without written permission from the author except for brief quotations within a review.

ISPN: 979-8-9863318-2-9 (print version)
979-8-9863318-3-6 (Ebook-Kindle version)

New York, NY / USA
Copyright © 2022 Chara Ann Tappin-McCabe

First Edition: June 2022
Author: Chara Ann Tappin-McCabe/CATappin

Cover art "Selfie from Hell" by GR167 Marked with Public domain Mark 1.0

Grateful Acknowledgement and Dedication is made to:

The wonderful teachers of Rainbow's End, Holly Wolf & Barbara Stern, who fanned the spark of creativity instilled by my wonderful parents and family, to my patient and endearing husband Stephen, my supportive and fellow bookworm siblings Colleen and Ashley, to Hermas Haynes, and Jill and Don Budnick, to my wonderful in-Laws, Phil and Robbie McCabe for their love, acceptance, hospitality, and unbridled sense of humor. And a special thanks to Sean Anderson and Pam Robertson Rivet, fellow authors who helped support and guide me through the grueling process of editing and publishing!

I write like my mother,

think like my father,

and am the continuation of my grandmothers' story.

To Angela, Trish, and Gale, my universal sisters; to Charlie, Uncles Tim, Paul, Don, James, Pandy, for their unending support, and to muses, past and present who inspired wonder and introspectiveness through adventure, misadventure, pain, and joy – never letting me forget, through an abundance of each, that we are all, in fact, human…imperfect, infallible, capable, and always evolving.

And lastly…to the unknown presence that haunts me

…until we are well met

Quickening/courtship/headfirst

"BEWARE of blind dates" by Atomic Mutant Flea Circus is licensed under CC BY 2.0. (Edited as Black and White Image)

The Mating Minuet

One step forward
two steps back
hands clasped, then not
turn and bow - *repeat.*

Fear, uncertainty, and phobias
maintain the tempo,
norms and expectations define the beat,
desire, acceptance, and need, haunt the melody,
while habit, intent and inconsistency infuse
the learned chorus.

Courtship

Caught on an urban hook.
A lovely day
An unexpected day
A breezy, bright, colorful, warm day
infused with newness and hope.

Mnemonic melodies shock and awe the senses,
climbing High,
dipping soulful and low,
ebbing and flowing with playful kinetic whimsy
like Pan in a Garden high on honey-suckled 'shrooms
or crackling grease on a worn ancient skillet.

Attuned to your vibe, your rhythm, your scent,
my body and mind leaden loadstones
turn with questions in mind,
slowly gauging, tasting the air,
pulled by your sweet mojo -
North's new abode?

Impromptu Picnic in Central Park

Impromptu picnic in Central Park,
from cotton candy in baby blues to royal speckled twilight,
multi-hued clouds flickered subliminal messages of myths and futures untold.

Wet Green air carried perfumed contemplation,
birthing colorful imaginings and wishful thinking,
while ritualistic contact through mishap and invitation,
desire and innovation,
broke the silence of things left unsaid.

Minstrel's lullabies set the primal hearts' pace,
as quickened bodies moved,
with the uncertain grace of those submerged
in instinct's murky resistance,
attraction's musty fragrant shroud,
quelled by common sense and truer aims,
mixed with the tangy odor of fear, expectation, and longing,
making opposition futile.

Wrapped in wool, perched on wet earth,
adventure evolved into comfort,
while staring at the stars silently toasting imagination,
they saluted the evening and prayed against familiarity,
in favor of maintaining the intimate's mystery a little longer.

Inner Child

Let's be children together.
Play every day in the
cloud speckled hues of Spring
Chew on sweet green grass and
Blow purple bubbles into the Wind.

Let's get dirty without a care,
wrestle on the wet April Earth
and Run Wild & wicked
through the Forest
Catching bugs in our mouths
while Skipping stones on serene and mirrored lakes.

Let's make mud pies with cherries on top,
Build sandcastles and move in,
Fly kites and take lessons.

Let's flatten coins on the tracks of life,
and dance over the premature graves
of those who've forgotten how.

Let's do it all.
Let's have fun,
and Spite the responsibilities of time!

The Kiss

Where has my breath gone?

To some place not quite forgotten,
purposefully dismissed into womb's oblivion
by a Will that commands dominion over Appetite?

To a place where a strategic kiss births inspiration
and foreplay's nativity requires exhibition?

To a place where lunar winds
cause the ebb and flow of coveted
adrenaline highs and lows?

Or...in your mouth, lost,
in Union's reflections and Cosmic Clicks?

Stung

Sitting here
Heart pounding
Anxiety overwhelms senses,
hands shaking
smiling reassuringly
while every muscle
Feels tight… taunt.

Ready for flight.
My lips, a meal,
as shallow breath escapes me,
and strange
yet all too familiar energies course
through my soul.

One a pining malcontent
Another sloven and base.
I am stilled,
and overpowered.

Intentions

What's left unsaid,
is left to be done,
things to be gained,
those to be won.

Intimacy

Intimacy
neither coerced nor expected,
neither reward nor boon,
like sweet breath,
is natural and essential...
until commoditized.

Love and Narcissism?

She wonders...

"If I say, *I love who I think you are*, does that make me narcissistic?"

Jumping in

Tie a string around it and
throw caution to the wind.

I will be our anchor and you the sail,
rising above obstacles cumulus and brume.

And with whispered prayers,
let the Gods' hands in fate,
guide us to journey's end.

Hopefully, together
I pray.

Casting Spells / addiction & submission / "first one's free, after that you gotta pay"

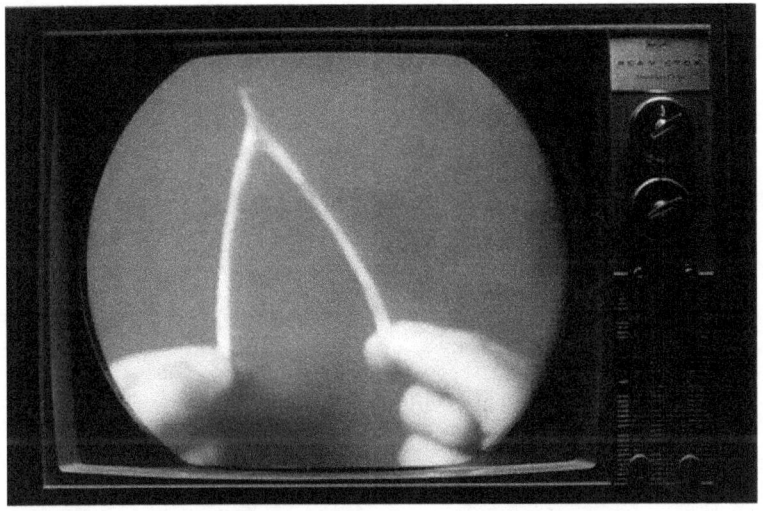

"careful what you wish for"
by woodleywonderworks is licensed under CC BY 2.0

A Lover's Prayer: Scene 1

Warm and Disarm me with Genuine smiles.
Tend my Heart carefully,
accept my affections given in kind,
Believe and Surrender.

For reasons unfathomable
our threads are tied - our story begun.
Attraction and Attachment,
Inevitable and Unavoidable.

The things I want, are words,
stuck in wombish buccal cavities,
and only my pen communicates freely,
those things only fugitively mouthed,
in the company of shadows,
where insecurities are masked in the gloom
and my smile mimics
subtle reflections of strength
greater than
I
in truth
Bare.

Inner Dialogue

Can I repeat during the day
that which should be whispered in the comfort of darkness?

Fondle you with velvet words.

Dare I think on you at night,
when sheer clouds cover the moon and stars flicker SOS?

Or should I attempt to point out the obvious,
that which could be said in a glance?
simply...
yes... and

Now...

Please.

Midnight "Cuddle"

Sincerity and kindness
Caused budding addiction.
Confessions of Love
Caused inner confliction.

The need of something warm and familiar
to cling closely to,
the need of a friendly face.

Thinking of You.

Dew and Eternity

Slept like a stone,
wishing you were
the sweet dewy moss and brush
beneath me.

Struck

So full of You
words will not come.
My tongue,
Swollen with emotion,
sticks in my throat,
while the Heart savors
what the mind has learned to Fear.

Hold and protect me,
and you will be loved beyond measure.

I will be your angelic djinn and you, my freedom
from a lamp of my own design.

You... my light
Me... your refuge.

Pheromone Highs

Eyes filled, glamor'd by decisions,
clouded by random choice and chance.

Lips and mouth await ravaging,
while the temple awaits the worshiper.

A quickened pulse pounds with fear, expectation and promise.

Breathless with wonder,
anticipating willful submission,
waxing and waning tidal thoughts overwhelm and
overcome Reason.

The mind whimpers wordless supplications for
joyful metamorphosis,
as the body cries to be consumed
and the soul quivers in anticipation of the union.

An Alpha's Respite

Feel me, Heal me.
Touch me, Hear me.
See me, Understand me.
Know me, Trust me.
Envelope me, Free me.
Pursue and Haunt me.
Master and Conquer me.

Overcome and Awe me into submission and
through masterful direction and tender administrations,
show me *Love*,
move me to *Surrender*,
Inspire me to *Trust*,
Comfort me unto *Release*.

A Novice's Trust

Relinquish control to expert, yet genteel administrations.
Embrace the exhilaration of restraint,
submit and exhale.

Be tantalized by the unfamiliar,
acknowledge the power of submission,
knowing only the worthy are permitted
to guide you through the unknown.

Find bliss in the release,
respite in the journey.

Spellbound

I stand,
addicted to your scent,
the wind... caressed by your music.
the night... ignited by your fire.
a wound... healed by your laughter.

You are nature incarnate,
and I,
a soul captured by your skillful web,
stand prepared to pay the cost,
for my willful entrapment,
the price,
such torment forever...

I pray.

Into the wind

Into the wind
I'd like to sing your name,
to await the tickling breeze's caress
and feel the warm breath of the sun,
sultry and seducing.

All elements,
answering on your behalf,
on a lovely green day,
when my thoughts
wander
across
You.

And when,
if in fevered bliss your name escapes my lips,
I shudder into wakefulness
yearning your spirit's return.

The Downwind Heart's Musings

What wounds drive you?
What needs stir you?

Every day,
In every way,
I am yours.

Putting down the mirror,
I wonder ... *do you feel loved*?

I would know your pain,
your story and dreams too.
I would know your soul,
I would know *You*.

The Narcissistic Obsessive

Let me climb you like a tree,
Wrap myself around your mind and
impregnate your thoughts,
until they give birth to
the only solution to the maddening
rush, thrill and demand
of your need...

Me.

Tap a Vein

I would
have you again,
with abandon and fixation.

I would
feed on your need,
and as masses undefined,
temporarily serviced,
watch
as we quiet our hidden Selves
and succumb to satiated slumber,
with dreams of the Unattainable.

Self-Destruction/payment due/Kali's banquet confessional

"the darkness falls"
Aimanness Photography is licensed under CC BY 2.0.

Personal Demons

Skipping to the rhythm hidden
between beats,
they frolic in the chaos,
gleefully welcoming portents of doom.

Watching and mocking us,
as we desperately seek the meter.

Beast of Burden

Give in to it.
Embrace it,
warm musty and tacky,
an entity unto itself,
Lust.

Granted entry on a pheromone cloud,
Ripe with slow thunderous burn and chimes,

Yet...
worthless unless
invited by love.

The Rite of Corruption

Where once convictions stood as armor
and shield against temptation,
a voluntary and vulnerable supplicant
Implored subjugation,
Today, she rejoices in freedom from accountability,
and taking delight in her corruption,
She is reborn.

Today, for good or ill, Ishtar has risen.
Let would-be paramours tremble!

Oh... Pretty One

Would be *"Cock of the Roost"*,
You strut around like a bedazzled peacock.
Witticisms and feathers tossed about like confetti,
A ticker-tape parade...theme music even,
all in an unfounded effort to make them want *You*.

Lured perhaps by the bright colors,
that genetic part which remains primal
invariably responds to your dance and more sheep are led
to psychic slaughter.

What species of animal are you?
Do you devour your mates,
leaving only haunted shells behind,
living animatronics testaments to your prowess?

Or

Do you lock them away,
as fleshy menageries,
broken toys in an under-lit shadowbox,
forgotten and dated suits in a misplaced closet,
your whimsical attentions,
while like a child, you look for your next new toy
forgetting,
one day you'll be too old to play,
and then what?

Once Wakened...Falsely

Once wakened in Love
yet loved Falsely,
she now awakens,
Irrelevant.

The Light neglected.
For want of steel, flint cannot alight.

Arrhythmia,
a discordant metronome,
reminds her...
it is not *Love* that is inconsistent,
but *Man*.

Fallacious Regret

Sly, Smooth, Silky mofo,
I know you. I wanted you. I had you.
Sitting alone, feeling a sack of used parts
I regret you.
Like a plague of locusts
a carousel of thoughts bombards me:

> "I didn't mean to make contact...should have avoided the trap, snaring me into a catatonic state of blissful denial! Stuck in our time, your story, making me reminisce the undone, the unsaid, and all sort of base bestial and vampiric things; shouldn't have let you touch me, quickening, like quick silver, the poison in my veins; Touch, Touch, T.O.U.C.H, suspended in time, molten lava touch, making my defenses steam like a fresh carcass. I shouldn't have displayed myself to your fleshy altar!"

With horrific and merciless clarity,
I confess I cannot honestly despair,
when after all the wet stiffness,
the fantasies didn't come true.
Now, in the aftershock, stewing in denial and guilt,
trying to convince myself I was an
"accidental" participant in my own demise,
capable of blaming no one,
despising my senses for their vivid recollections and torment,
I cringe from the me,
that embraced the Devil,
and Liked it!!

Yesterday's Blue Plate Special

Sitting here...
failing the stoic expression,
playing at normalcy,
seemingly interested in the present,
I think...
on fruits recently consumed,
aptly cored,
and likewise dismissed.

Cavity

I close my eyes to block out the sight of you.
Plug my ears, so I can't hear you.
But I am filled with you, nonetheless.

My core etched,
vibrates with the Knowledge of *You,*
like the dull throb of a sugar filled Cavity.

Tantrum

*"Wither to your touch
repulsed by your stare,
your enticing deformities afflict
nightmarish images in my mind.
Every moment spent together,
spent in false adoration and herculean tolerance.
I loathe you!"*

Through my lids,
these hateful words said,
else I be betrayed.

Exorcism

To repel that which has been stealthily insinuated into me,
Implanted senses with sentimental gore,
I strike!
I Act!

Pulling at the asphyxiating stale gummy bear substance
cemented around my organs, my nostrils, my teeth, my lungs,
my mouth, my heart.

Gagged and gagging,
I pull out the tacky stuff,
stuff
stuff
stuff
baggage
taunt and insistent,
disabled from laughing or crying.

"Will" meant little, exercised in vain,
against your sworn disposition and charms.

Now stuck in a piteous state of self-loathing
and anger born from deception,
I strive to Strike out,
at all that was birthed in my mind's eye with your introduction,
in the hopes of obliterating
the Memory of you.

Purge

Purge!
Purge!
Purge!

My wretched pen chokes on words I cannot perform.
Myself, my guilt, my passions, my only audience.
My mind, this white glaring page, my amphitheater,
where doubts and avoided confessions
echo ceaselessly and mercilessly,
off defensive canyon walls that conspire against me.

Purge the thoughts, Perish the deed!

The power of *"The Word"*, words
shadow ghouls of the Eighth Circle
leave me both tattered and shamed by my passive inactivity,
and heartened by my silence.

Disengaged

I am present,
but
unbound,
unbridled,
untamed,
unfazed,
unamazed and
disenchanted.

Understand this,
your script,
holds no interest for me.

Been there, done that.

Again

Shuddered breath meets a shaken disposition,
as the mind wonders whether the Center will Hold,
a stoic witness mourns respite's retreat,
while consistency threatens acceptance.

Missing that Thang

I miss that *Thang,*
That *Spark*, that *Chemistry,*
That *VIBE,*
that made it all seem so real, so plausible, so possible,
that *"Zip, Bang, Pow, Snap, Crackle & Pop!"*
that made it all seem so right,
that welcoming warm and fuzzy *"mellow yellow"*
final *"Ahhhh"*, perfectly mated union *"Click"!*

And most of all,
I miss that,
"roll over in the middle of the night,
reach out and spoon you" Pacifier,
that made me Dream of
More.

Adrift

A broken load stone will lead you North,
no more than a wounded heart will speak on joy.
No words...
Odysseus adrift...Penelope abandoned.

Better a castaway, on dry land, where barren consistency
lends itself to numbing complacency,
than adrift in a sea, where tumultuous waves
simulate life and false hope glimmers on the horizon.

The Aids Test

Here on this index finger,
this funny little prick
stands judge and jury,
adjourned to decide the caliber of my fate.
The pricked muted witness barks tauntingly
with purposeful intent.

Can my body's temperament belie health,
for that matter exaggerate ill?

Body and Mind joined in reluctant alliance,
communicate no collective understanding,
except to inform that fear betrays acceptance.

One way or the other
I will Live.

Not Juliette

She held her breath too long.
Turning blue,
she faded away into a discordant melody,
waiting to be discovered by a writer of Love songs,
"waiting for a girl like you".

A Muse wasted,
she held her breath too long,
and Died …
unremarked and unnoticed.

Don't go/Hard Conversations/...till soon is now/lonely

"The Truth Of Being A Highly Sensitive Person . Katie Kuo"
by POET ARCHITECTURE is marked with CC PDM 1.0

Catch & Release

Your freedom I would offer,
if it were mine to command,
'though without guarantee or map,
authored by fate, predicting favorable futures.

Promises and fortitude are never,
uncompromised by *Time*.

So… as one of nature's creatures
I submit to its order.

the translucent contract remains
clouded by human intellect,
the heart remains Base, being all that remains Simple,
while the *Will*,
evolves from both natural and man-made constructs.

We are as free as we can be…
and freer still, some believe,
when we find
The *"One"*.

This Silence

There is silence ….

Comforting and pacific,
the sort born of familiarity and contentment,
a still balm on the soul of its occupants,
twins in the womb,
embraced by unspoken understanding and
congenial acceptance.

And then there is *Silence*…

Deafening disconcerting and calamitous,
filled with a kinetic lethal psychic Noise,
Ripe with Fears spawned from the Unknown,
an endless abyss of cerebral monstrosities,
creeping, lithe, and sharp things,
crawling from the dark side of
Pavlovian lessons learned…unintentionally.

Sitting in proximity, yet worlds apart,
I can't help but wonder,
mental fly swatter in hand,

… which silence is *This*?

Let's Talk

Suspecting what one won't know,
fearing what the other can't,
whose voice do they choose,
in the dark crevices of their minds?

Experience does not prophecy make,
nor does willful blindness,
guarantee resolution.

Heads buried in the sand,
mouths muted and bound,
hearts not necessarily wounded,
as the carousel turns
turning
driven by anxiety or someone's truth untold.

Misunderstanding the understanding or
understanding the misunderstanding
bodies vibrate and twist,
pulse and turn,
mechanical and discordant,
the unknown remaining a matter of debated certainty,
while cowardice prevents the actors from saying,

"STOP
...*can we talk*"?

Rumors of "Too Late"

You never told me you dreamed
of green meadows, blue skies
of home-coming August joys
and what could have been.

We never shared heart-filled moments,
without some overhanging shadow lurking in our minds,
putting our hearts in separate bonds... shackled.

When fate saw fit to give us the keys,
like children in the dark,
we wandered in opposite directions.

Given light, we saw each other for the first time,
strangers in love with what had until now been left to the imagination.

We never went camping,
or basked in the summer sun.
We never saw beauty together,
and
We never danced.

Is it too late?

Satellite

Looking at earth's reflection on the dark side of the moon,
I swallowed your pride.

A satellite;
Anywhere I would have followed you,
But seasons, with your orbit, changed.

You should know what you're running from.

Epiphany

Either accompanied and alone, or
just
Alone.
Better the latter,
than burdened by disappointment,
in those you hoped would fill the void.

Children of Divorce

Tongue tied
by semantics
history and intentions.

It's hard to be a Bridge,
when Both sides are Burning.

… what more can be said?

Reluctant Sentinel

Neither want,
nor need,
nor think you deserve.
Simply be...
exist and observe.

The child in the corner sees all.

Taught to Covet

I suffered from some indecision about the finality of things...

Why do we always want passionately those things beyond our reach - when in fact, if segregated from the imagined possibilities or instituted barriers we learn, we no longer *know* if we want these things intrinsically, in and of themselves?

Once removed... independent of any action on my part, I find
these misgivings vanquished and certainty
is encapsulated in the loss.

Keep Your Promises

A lot can happen,
Between
Now and
Again.

A Silent Prayer

I hear whispers of your song,
echoed in my heart,
and pray the lyrics are the same.

Errant thought of Loves Long Past

I tried to hold

you,

but

my wounds

…. got in the way.

My Pieta

Where a part of your soul has lost a limb,
an awkward and hallow gait,
a phantom of fulfillment,
haunts the memory of journeys once shared.

Such limbs cannot be replaced,
only buried under new joys,
if luck prevails.

Today, I shed an unexpected tear,
as remembrance surfaced
of once shared mirth.

I held the wound,
my pieta
and thought of you.

Ancient Witness

Still as a glacier,
awaiting the Breezes' news of
Spring's fever,
Winter's madness,
Summer's love and
Fall's gladness.

Next life

Still... looking for your soul,

in the faces of those I might learn to love

...waiting for the Guff to tip.

Before I die

You have only to
touch me,
look upon me.
Kiss me Quick!
Before my heart beats its last,
and I will
Awaken
Invigorated, Enlivened,
Invulnerable and Reborn

And... still,
If that last breath should yet come,
bidden by unyielding Fate,
I will master Time and
Will it to linger but a moment longer,
as a murmur in the breeze,
a Spell cast,
for Reunion in the next life,
and a Prayer for you in this one.

Regrets, Requests & Remembrance

Having caused this,
let me not die twice,
but say my name,
thru the ages.
For I would live again,
if only as syllables upon your lips.

Piously Coveting

Stolen glances fugitively wonder *"what if?"*.
While duty requires shackled tongues,
let us simply,
Know
and be contented with that.
... 'till and if *"when"* and *"what"* becomes *"now"*,
in this life or the next.

Au revoir ....

    till soon is now,
    till hope is certainty,
    and dreams are memories.

Ignore me

Do not listen to me,

for my Words are Corrupt

with the Need for Love.

Redemption/gratitude/obligatory confessions

Maghera Caves, Ireland, 2022

Introductions unnecessary

How do I *know* you... *remember* you, you ask?
How could I not...
when I was on you, with you, in you, of you.
You were I,
and me was we,
and all was divine,
both before and after the veil,
at the first, the last breath, reborn.

I've known you through the Cycles of Time,
and awaited you anew in each.

Husband

While physical exhaustion erodes her joie de vivre,
and familial challenges and debilitating illnesses
hit those she loves.
While sleeplessness and psychic fatigue leave her
heart sick and stuck
on a scratched record of her own
inner dialogue of growing fears,
you remain near and dear,
her rock... her refuge in the eye of the storm.

Dependable and present,
a constant Friend and Companion.

Know that with love she silently thanks you for
your unconditional love and support.
A verdant balm for a scorched soul.

Nexus

What is *"time"*,
when each conscious breath is a sweet reminder
that your affections envelop me,
when only fear of losing you
catches the Breath, holding it Ransom,
for a Prayer?

You are Tranquility, Salvation...Source & Answer.
Don't you know that you are my *Sun*?

My *Ra*...
With you, the gift is life.

Without it, contradiction.

Happy Anniversary

Another year has passed,
sparks, flashes and quiet moments,
every holiday, every moment,
shared laughs and tears,
dreams and fears,
a string of lights,
leading from recognition...
to you...
to home.

A Woman's Smile

Fulfilling her duty...
she lit her candle

... and the sun rose.

An Author's Confession

Empathy to the *Reader*, the burden of having to read and in so doing, the opportunity to repeat the endeavor endlessly in search of comprehension, lends itself to obsession and instability.

The *Reader* is required and unkindly directed, to assign temper, tone, and motive to words and turns of phrase written with purposeful ambiguity...cursed to forever wonder at the Author's intent and blanching at the inequities of the same.

The *Author* has but two hurdles to overcome before the deed is done: first, to muster the courage to commit intent to paper and, and secondly, to have the audacity to publish and promote said letters.

Once committed, the precise words fade from memory, the confession completed and bound, the writer's mind, thus purged and assuaged, is clear and all that remains are vague impressions of intent, forgotten reason and creativity's psychic afterbirth.

The *Reader's* obligation, once committed, is to read the piece in its entirety and hope for satisfaction and understanding – while the *Author* accepts the first and prayers for the later.

Thank You

It was a daunting step out of the artists' proverbial closet – to be brave enough to publish – so first and foremost... thank you for your support and taking the time to read some of my work.

Like many, I write as a means of cathartic release... to purge the thoughts in my head - whether birthed from my own experiences or from observations of the experiences of others and the world around me. My *"Inner Dialogue"* has always been a constant bombardment of thoughts, questions and yes, even debate – demanding acknowledgement and release.

In today's *"modern"* and seemingly *"advanced"* world, we suffer under a constant barrage of input. We are so distracted by the external, we've learned to fear the *"mirrors"* that provide the opportunity look into and know our *"selves"*.

So, I say *WRITE! DRAW! CREATE!*

Vent the thoughts and questions in your heart and mind... give birth to something and blossom.

About the Author

Born in 1970, Chara Ann Tappin lives in New York City with her exceptionally patient and loving husband, Stephen, and perfectly adorable dog, *"Gizzie the Biscuit"* a.k.a. *"sock thief extraordinaire"*.

Born and raised in the heart of New York, she attended schools in Brooklyn, New York, and Sweden. She studied History, Philosophy and the Arts at Hunter College and makes a hobby of studying other languages. Growing up, she was fascinated by religion, archeology, and dance, all of which lent themselves to the development of introspection and imagination.

When not writing, she spends much of her time working, traveling to visiting family far and wide, reading, writing, daydreaming of a *"Gene Roddenberry-esque"* future, collecting stones, and hugging trees.

She is steadily collecting material for what she hopes will be her next two projects- *"Shakespeare on the Corner of East 11th Street"* and *"A Philosophy of Stone"*..

Books by Chara Ann Tappin

<u>Inner Dialogue Series</u>

"Inner Dialogue" (Book 1)

"Love Lost & Other Monsters" (Book 2)

www.ingramcontent.com/pod-product-compliance
Lightning Source LLC
Chambersburg PA
CBHW071229160426
43196CB00012B/2458